TRANQUIL
Infinity

SALLY-ANN CHARNOCK

BALBOA.
PRESS
A DIVISION OF HAY HOUSE

Balboa Press books may be ordered through booksellers or by contacting:

Balboa Press
A Division of Hay House
1663 Liberty Drive
Bloomington, IN 47403
www.balboapress.com.au
1-(877) 407-4847

ISBN: 978-1-4525-0624-1 (sc)
ISBN: 978-1-4525-0625-8 (e)

Because of the dynamic nature of the Internet, any web addresses or links contained in
this book may have changed since publication and may no longer be valid. The views
expressed in this work are solely those of the author and do not necessarily reflect the
views of the publisher, and the publisher hereby disclaims any responsibility for them.

The author of this book does not dispense medical advice or prescribe the use of any
technique as a form of treatment for physical, emotional, or medical problems without the
advice of a physician, either directly or indirectly. The intent of the author is only to offer
information of a general nature to help you in your quest for emotional and spiritual well-
being. In the event you use any of the information in this book for yourself, which is your
constitutional right, the author and the publisher assume no responsibility for your actions.

Any people depicted in stock imagery provided by Thinkstock are models,
and such images are being used for illustrative purposes only.
Certain stock imagery © Thinkstock.

Printed in the United States of America

Balboa Press rev. date: 07/18/2012

Dedication

This book is dedicated to my son, Guy Oliver Charnock.

"And I would wait a lifetime
To see you smile again
And maybe on the other side
We will re-connect"

Maor Levi

Introduction

This world is a realm of dreams, hopes and infinite possibilities. Each of us has our own purpose, our own path. As we journey through our own unique sadness and joy, we hold within our hearts the goodness of eternity.

Follow your heart as you journey with me through each poem and discover hidden meanings within your soul. Let your inner light shine through as you find inspiration and become love itself. I decided to put my collection of poems together after my son passed away in early March 2012. These poems were inspired from love and an inner knowledge that we can do anything.

Whilst travelling overseas my eldest son Guy was involved in an accident that left him in a coma. My husband and I flew over to be with him as soon as we heard. Initially we were told that things were looking very positive and he soon started to show signs of recovery. Unfortunately within the first week he suffered another unexpected trauma which set back his recovery. It was a harsh blow since just the day before he had managed to spell out "I luv u" on a piece of paper we had given him.

For the next few weeks we stayed by his side, ever hopeful, during which time we were told it could be months before he would wake up. Our three other children had stayed behind in Melbourne, and we soon had to fly back to be together as a family. It was one of the hardest things to leave him, but there was nothing more we could do at that stage but be together, strong in our unity as a family. Over the next few months we flew over several times to be with him, and were lucky enough to have friends and family visiting to support us and keep him company.

Sadly due to the complications of his condition, Guy passed away in early March 2012. The hope we had kept alive for months was extinguished and, at the age of just twenty two, my eldest son was no longer with us. My journey has been recorded here within these poems.

I am very grateful to my whole family and dedicate this book to my son. We are connected in death as we were in life. Guy, your eternal love and energy surrounds and flows through me. It has given me the strength to accept your soul's journey. This part was a gift to us, the next is a gift to you.

Time places me nowhere,
For now I have reached
The place where I begin.

The need to write
Is here with me now,
The words
Spilling out onto the paper.

Time places me here
With you, reading
My words written
At the end of the beginning.

Once I Was a Writer

Once I was a writer.
Once I was a poet;
Once, an artist.

As droplets of rain
Fall from
Sun-drenched skies,
I am reborn
To that life
Once more.

I capture my dreams—
Soft whispers of love.
Miracles of motherhood,
Friendship, lust,
And death.

Colours imagined
From palette to canvas,
Framed by soft light,
Tones of palest blue
And delicate whites
Create a picture as pure
As love
Imprinted on my soul.

Once I was a writer.
Once I was a poet;
Once, an artist.
I am now reborn
To that life
With light and ease,
With laughter and love,
With forgiveness
And grace.

Peacefulness

Breath
Takes time,
Fresh air
Into your lungs.
Rest your head.
Let the world
Carry on
While you are
Alone with
Your thoughts.

As if for the first time,
Let your ears
Hear the birds.
Drop your eyelids,
And let them be still.
Allow yourself to
Relax;
Slowly
Unwind.
Feel free
As you find
Inner peace,
Stillness.
Just be.
Rejuvenate.

Outside In

The world is
Outside me,
Yet I see my world
From within.

How easy it is to
Believe in yourself
From the inside,
Yet how hard
From the outside
Looking in.

I feel free to
Bare my love
As I look
Outward to the
Skies beyond.

How easy it is
To believe in yourself
From the inside,
Yet how hard
From the outside.

Thinking,
Reflecting:
As it burns my heart,
I learn to share
My inner thoughts.

The red sun is my soul.
Starbursts of light
Shine everlasting love
Upon my world.

I am wisdom.
I am whole.
I am complete.

I have brought the world
Inside.
I have shared
A part of me,
Shared my life
With those I love.
I have gained wisdom.
I have gained strength
From outside in.

I am wisdom.
I am whole.
I am complete.

Gift of Self

The art of who we are,
The essence of our being
Is in the giving.

Those who do not give
Will never experience
The beauty
Within the canvas,
As the brush dances
Delicately
Over its simple plane,

Creating
An exceptional
Gift of self.

No Need to Rush

I don't want to rush
A rare glimpse of
Solitude;
I actually live here
On this
Island of green.

Listening to the birds,
Watching the water
Glistening and rippling
As the breeze
Flows through my hair,

Taking in all of
My surroundings:
Beauty
In its purest form.
A rare glimpse
Of solitude.
No need to rush.

So I sit.
I write amongst
Native plants,
Swans gliding,
Reflections
Shimmering
Violet in the lake,
Lovers strolling,
Children playing,

Lonely souls
Gathering
Their thoughts
Whilst giggling girlfriends
Picnic on the spring grass.
Time out for us all
In the daisy chain of life.

Look for Today, Not Tomorrow

Search the sky,
For the light is dim
Though the light
Wants to shine.

Look for today,
Not tomorrow,
For each breath
Is a promise of life,
Each smile
A promise of love,
And each thought
A mystery
Waiting to unfold.

Across the Miles

Across the miles
From the shores
Of time
Our hearts
Meet again.

I look at the map of life.
Journeys travelled
Through days of rain,
Nights of thunder,
And blue skies
Cloudless and bright.

Hearts join
As stories unfold;
Tears are shed,
Forming rainbows
Of laughter and sadness.

The waters of life
Flow freely
Across the shores
Of time, as our hearts
Meet again.

Into the Light

Out of the darkness
Comes warmth,
A blanket wrapped
Around the soul:
Closeness
Known only to you.

Into the light
Comes a friendship
Sealed for life,
A gift of listening:
An understanding
Of the journey ahead.

Out of the darkness
Steps an angel:
A spirit of love
Known only to you.

A familiar face,
A warm smile,
A voice of reason,
A person who cares.

Out of the darkness
Comes our awakening;
A time to shine
And heal our broken hearts.

Out of the darkness
Comes love
So powerful
It turns to light,
Shimmering
In the night.

Time for Myself

At one with self:
Steam rises,
Hypnotic candle,
Rhythm of breath
With each exhale,
Relaxing.

Then,
Tears flow.
I see prisms of light
Twisting, turning,
Popping
As each droplet falls.

Beauty of sadness
Brings joy.
As I let go,
I stretch from
Being curled up.
I am flowing,
Feminine,
Delicate.

I feel my spirits lifting
As my soul revives,
And I am once again
At one with myself,
Taking time
For myself.

To Love

To love is to know.
To feel is to think.
To be is to imagine
Beyond anything
You could ever dream.

The sea is eternal.
The sky is the light.
The moon is our other side.

Feelings run deep,
Whilst words merely
Touch the surface.

The Art of Friendship

The colours of love
Create a waterfall
Of happiness.
To care for
Someone else
Completes the picture
Painted in one's eye.

To give is to find
A piece of jigsaw
Of oneself,
To reach out
And say you are there.
This is the true
Art of friendship.

Floating Away Far Yonder

Have you ever felt
As though your life
Was floating away, far yonder?

As the sun sets,
The warmth
Turns to an icy chill.
Tears form:
Frustration,
Anger,
Love;
But most of all,
Sadness.

I tell you
Your heart will mend
On the evening breeze.
You will feel
The whispers of love;
The sun will rise again.

Once more, you will feel
The earth's warmth.
Guided by angels,
Your heart will mend
As you float away
On the clouds, far yonder.

Open Your Eyes

The time to start is now.
Lasting forever
Into the nights of summer
And the days of winter,
Across the borders
Of our time,
Into the horizons
Of the unknown world.

Water like silk
Washes over you,
Glistening in the
Tranquillity
Of our minds.

Do not resist
Floating in the
Dimension of change,
Or letting go of the
Fabric of existence.

Be still a moment.
Feel the very breath
Of life.
Open your eyes,
And your heart
Shall be free.

Fly and Be Free

Exotic madness fills my lungs.
Laughing out loud,
I feel his love,
Full of enchantment and promise.

Moments are lost in time
As I take in his warmth.
I become dizzy with love,
Momentarily forgetting
Where I am.

He fills my heart with joy.
He lifts my spirits.
Fly and be free.
There are no limitations,
No boundaries;
Just clear skies
And a gentle, warm breeze.

Angel of love, fly with me.
Upon the canvas of life
Images unfold,
Layer after layer,
As the painting of self
Is revealed.

I have found freedom.
Like the artist's impression,
I am all colours,
I am light and texture,
Creating a masterpiece
To journey's end and beyond.

Everyone Is an Artist . . . Even You

I am the artist
Who never was.
I am opening up
From the inside out,
Drawing
From the centre
The colours of my core.
I see in images;
I write in feelings;
I create from my soul.

We all need ourselves.
I know;
I understand;
I have learnt
Who I am in life.
I found a small part of myself
By unravelling the enormity
Of my existence,
And realised
We are all artists,
We all create;
It is part of being.

You are the artist
Who never was,
Opening up
From the inside out,
Unravelling
The enormity
Of your existence.

The Page

Tried to think,
Mind blank,
Pen poised
Over expressionless paper,
Waiting . . .
Watching as imaginary ink
Drips onto my manuscript—
Drip, drip—
Misplaced letters
Becoming a mass
Of sticky black ink
Belching their mockery
At my failing.
I looked away
In the distance.
Turning back,
I saw
A blank page.
No words;
Just neat lines
Flirting with me.
Tentatively,
I touched the virgin paper.
I began to write,
Filling the page,
Then another,
On and on
Into the night,
Until at last,
Deed done,
I was finished.

No One Knows

What we feel
As thoughts,
In letters,
Flash by,
Come and go,
Come and go.
Visualise those
Demons,
Let the storm rage.
The pain is real;
Accept

Hear the sounds,
Shut out the noise;
Breath
Fading to nothingness,
Silence.

Don't push me away;
Find a place for me.
I am here with you.

Look how far I have come.
Challenge how far I will go
By living my moment,
This moment.
Now
Look into my eyes,
See my soul.
You understand;
You truly know.

How Do We Love?

How do we love?
With passion that runs so deep,
Waters that never run dry,
Crisp, white skies—
The palest hint of blue
In an open expanse
Like tears
Of sadness
Dropping into the ocean of life—

We sometimes feel alone;
But never just one soul,
For the ocean and sky
Encompass all that is.

So peaceful, so beautiful,
We live on,
Souls of energy
Through our deepest love
With passion that runs deep,
And waters that never run dry.

Pam's Garden

You are a garden
Of love:
Your petals are
Delicate,
Your leaves
Gently sway
In the breeze.

You are care
Woven between
Blades of grass.
Your roots are
Rich in growing
Friendship.

Your nature
Harmonises
With the birds,
And care is
Seeded
In your earth.

Breathing in
Delights
The senses,
And your warmth
Shines through
As you grow
Into a beautiful
Place to be.

Amber Well-Being

I stir the amber liquid,
Watching the steam rise.
I stir the amber liquid
And watch the world
Swim by.
I stir the amber liquid
And find stillness
Within the storm.
Alone in my thoughts,
Sinking lower,
I see an opening of light
Appear out of the dark skies;
A feeling of unrest,
A ray of hope,
A feeling of happiness
As clouds race by.
More love, less doubt;
More hope, less sorrow.

The amber liquid's warmth
Trickles slowly
Down my throat
As I drink in
Well-being.
The sun shines
Through open clouds.
So much better—
I feel
So much better,
Finding stillness
Within the storm.

Footprints

As the dawn breaks
And the day begins,
I see a path
I need to travel.

Long nights
Followed by short days,
Footprints lasting
Forever.

Tears fall
As he gently touches
My hand;
I feel his strength.
Seeing through
The dark night,

My journey
Continues.
Not knowing
Where
It will take me,

With every breath
I take another step,
Leaving footprints
Of my life.

Secrets

If you listen very hard,
You will hear the secrets
Being told.

If you listen very hard,
You will gain knowledge,
Truth, and understanding.

If you listen very hard
For meaning more powerful,
You acquire a taste for life
More powerful
Than the spoken word;
A deeper desire,
An inner clarity.

If you listen very hard,
You will hear
All there is to hear.

Entwined for All Eternity

Today in the tranquil
Oasis of my world,
I feel protected by the
Spirits around me.

I know I will be safe
Once I leave this world
And pass to the next;
I will be with those
Who truly love me,
For each spirit has many lives—
This is but one.

For those with me today,
I will be here always.
As my light shines for you
And my soul wraps around yours,
Our pure energy and love
Entwine for all eternity.

Today I Found My Tears

Today I found my tears,
No words;
Just tears.

Relief,
Sheer relief:
He is back
From his dream state
Of unconsciousness,
A place of no thought.

I cried away my sadness,
I left behind my weariness
Just for a moment.
Instead,
I gave my love to my son.
I found a way to tell him
How amazing he really is.
His strength, his love, my love
Shuts out, closes off
The reality of today
And creates a safe connection
Between us, child and parent,
Mother and son.

We are bound,
Not by tubes or wires,
But by our inner knowing
That we each exist.
We are one another's strength
For this moment, for every moment.

Silent Tears

We shed silent tears,
Smiling, overjoyed,
Exchanging knowing looks.
His bright blue eyes
Not really aware,
Not understanding.
Recognise our faces.
"Mum and Dad"
His ears hear our
Familiar soothing voices.

As no words could sound,
With pen and paper
He carefully spelt out
"I luv u."
His kiss on my cheek,
Dry and shaky,
Grabbed my heart;
His hug, warm and close.

Then tiredness overtook him,
His weary body
Falling back into a
Dreamless state of coma.

Hope Belongs Here

I feel him.
I know him.
He is strong.
He is with us.

I feel I might lose him.
How hard that is for a mother.
He talks to me,
Some days telling me
How hard it is for him,
Other days telling me
It's going to be okay.

"It's all going to be okay, Mum."

I want him back.
I need him to come back to us.

What can I do
Besides be a good mother,
Be here for my other two sons
And for my daughter? My husband
Stay strong for them, for us,
For Guy.

Be together.
There is a flow from
Earth's core to
Beyond our realms.
He is in between,
But strongly connected.

Life is so Fragile

Gentle soul,
Be kind to me.
Life is so fragile,
Like rose petals
Dropping
One by one
From the dying flower.
Soft Earth,
Cushion my fall
As I lie down
To watch the
Clouds of my life
Float by.
The whispering wind
Chills my thoughts.
I feel lost
In this universe of uncertainty.
Make me believe once more
In unconditional love.
My tears dampen
The rich soil beside me,
Nourish the roots of life
And feed the earth once more.

Rainwater

The rain
Comes down,
The water of life
Drains away
Into the soil of death.

Yet seeds
In the soil
Form new life
Once more,
The soil of
Life and death.

Water of life:
Tears of
Great sadness
And pain.

His tears
Become mine,
And the water
Becomes a river
Upon which I
Sail away.

Mirror Image

Life can be flat,
A plateau of sadness;
Feelings numbed,
Just an air of uncertainty.

Clouds float by,
Rain comes and goes.
The sun shines
Without warming
My skin.

I am here, present.
My mirror image is
Over there with him,
Touching his skin, his hair,
Watching his face,
Whispering to his soul.

My son,
My dear beloved son,
Come back to us.

I love you.
We all love you.
Dream of us
And come home.

I Will Not Forget You

I am so sad,
So uncertain
As I contemplate
What will not be.

I cling to memories,
Making them appear
In my mind.
"I will not forget you,"
I scream in my head.
Yet I am so afraid I will.

Broken,
I feel numb
As I try to pick up
The pieces of our
Shattered lives.

I look at my children,
Wondering
What it will be like,
Knowing
Our world is unbalanced.

I look at my husband
And see his pain,
Which reflects my own.

I listen to the rain,
I feel the sun on my face,
And hear my son
Whispering his love
For me, for us.

I understand
With time we will
Accept his death
As part of life,
But for now, I ache.
For now, I cry.

Behind the Door of Life

You have come to me
From the far side,
Your love flowing
Through me.

I hear you,
I feel you,
I see you not,
But I love you always.

Why are you back?
Do you miss me?
Did I hear you calling?
Did I feel you reach out
Behind the door of life
Sealed shut until I take
My last breath?

I know you are there.
I will join you in time.
My love,
Be patient.
I hear you,
Feel you,
See you not,
But love you
Always.

Sing For Me

There is a time
When I need you here,
Beside me still,
When the waves
Cease,
The wind drops,
And the world sleeps.

A time when
The stars are out,
And the sky is dark,
And the sea is
Deathly quiet.

Sing for lost love.
To hear your voice
Is to heal my soul.
There is music in my heart
When I feel your presence.

There is a time
When I need you here.
Sing for me
Once more
Beside me still,
When the waves
Cease,
The wind drops,
And the world sleeps,
My Child of Love,
My Child of Love.

Days and nights
Will go by,
My love for you
Never wavering.
To me you will
Always be
My Child of Love,
My lovable guy,
The one who made us laugh,
The one who made us care.

Silent Moments

My world without you:
Silent moments,
Times of sadness.

My world without you:
Thoughtful moments,
Times of grief.

My world with your spirit:
Laughter and fun,
Creative moments,
Words of love.
Beside me, joyous spirit:
Silent moments.

Then one day I Realised

Time goes by.
Pain is healing,
Love is deep.
Sadness
Now entwined with joy
As the memories are held
Locked inside my heart.

Time to think,
Time to write
The words inside my soul.
Time to face myself,
Those I love, and see
The mirrors of life;
Love reflecting
Ad infinitum.

Time to care
For those close,
Guiding them with light.
Move forward,
Forward in the spirit of love,
With a heart full of forgiveness.
Walk along the shore of time
Into a cloudless sunset,
As the world spins round
And time lasts forever.

Love is not Lost, but Found

In our lives,
Never forgotten:
The joy we had
When you were near.

In everything I do,
You are present.
The wound of death
Will heal;
Music will play
And laughter will fill the air.
Tides will ebb and flow.
Shells, like pearls,
Will appear in fine sand.

Colour will be in my life
On a summer's breeze
When the sun goes down,
On a winter's cold night
When the rains fall,
And your rainbow spirit shines.

You will be there
When I fall,
Your presence felt,
Your messages seen.
Encouraging whispers
Will be heard
As I live my life
Without you.

I love you
For eternity;
I will miss you forever.
You are locked
Deep within my heart
With precious memories
And future adventures.
As we sail the oceans of time
And feel the thrills of life,
You will be with me
Always.

One Door Shuts, Another Opens

As the door opens,
Take that road,
A new direction;
Walk through
With confidence.

Ask what you feel,
Question your doubts,
Answer yourself justly,
For now is the time.

The door is open;
Walk through
And you will find
What inspires your heart
And feeds your soul.

Home Once More

I am the water,
I am the sand,
I am the pebble
You turn over in your hand.
I am the shells
Washed in, washed out.
I am the light glistening on the sea,
I am the clouds,
I am the bird
Soaring high, dipping low.
I am the warmth in the sun,
I am the gentle breeze
Whispering past your face.
I am the rocks near
The dunes beyond,
And the beach as far
As the eye can see.
I am the waves crashing
One after another.
I am all the sounds you hear,
I am the silence you need,
I am the footprints
You make and leave behind.
I am the memories you have,
I am the ocean of tranquillity,
I am home once more.

Infinite Love

Asking me
To follow him,
Asking me
To trust him,
He took hold
Of my hand.
I felt his happiness;
I felt so willing
To follow,
Excited,
As his joy spread
Through me.

He led;
I followed
Into the light.
Merging,
Weightless,
Vivid colours,
No substance;
Just energy,
The feeling of oneness.
I became him,
And he me.
We were the universe;
We were pure energy,
Beautiful spirits
Merged with
The white light,
Pure,
Free,
Weightless.
I was so
Deliriously happy.

His energy glowed.
He told me
This is where he belongs.
He wanted me to see
How wonderful it was.

I was so blessed
To be there,
To feel universal,
To understand,
To have a glimpse
Of what he knew:
Pure love
Radiating out.

I knew I needed to go.
Feeling torn,
I wanted to stay,
But I knew
It was not to be.
I said I had to go;
It was not my time.
He knew,
He understood.
I felt so blessed to
See for myself
His excitement
To be in the light.
He led me back,
Thanking me for
Trusting him.

I knew then
He was staying there,
Yet my mind
Locked it away
Until another time.
Until I chose
To understand
His presence,
His message of
Infinite love,

I had found his
Tranquil infinity.

Printed in the United States
By Bookmasters